International Research to Monitor Sustainable Forest Spatial Patterns: Proceedings of the 2005 IUFRO World Congress Symposium

Editors:

Kurt H. Riitters, Deputy Program Manager
U.S. Department of Agriculture Forest Service
Foresty Sciences Laboratory
Research Triangle Park, NC 27709

and

Christine Estreguil, Scientific Officer
European Commission, DG – Joint Research Centre
Institute for Environment and Sustainability
Land Management and Natural Hazards Unit
Ispra, Italy

CONTENTS

INTERNATIONAL RESEARCH TO MONITOR SUSTAINABLE FOREST SPATIAL PATTERNS

Kurt Riitters and Christine Estreguil[1]

INTRODUCTION

Presentations from the symposium "International Research to Monitor Sustainable Forest Spatial Patterns," which was organized as part of the International Union of Forest Research Organizations (IUFRO) World Congress in August 2005, are summarized in this report. The overall theme of the World Congress was "Forests in the Balance: Linking Tradition and Technology," and the symposium addressed the Congress sub-theme "Demonstrating Sustainable Forest Management." There is a long forestry tradition of site-specific management of forest spatial patterns to enhance wildlife habitat, water quality, recreation experience, and other forest amenities. But, there is not a long history of experience in national and continental reporting of forest spatial pattern as an indicator of biodiversity. As a result, research is needed to understand how to measure, monitor, interpret, and report on forest spatial patterns in relation to biodiversity at multiple scales ranging from countries to continents. The purpose of the symposium was to review recent international experiences with a view towards identifying research priorities.

The contributors to this report operate within international frameworks that guide assessments of forest spatial patterns. The Ministerial Conference on the Protection of Forests in Europe (MCPFE) involves 44 countries and functions as a platform for science and policy dialog and cooperation to sustain forest biodiversity (MCPFE 2005). The 2005 MCPFE Work Programme recommends criteria and indicators for conservation and sustainable management of forests, including indicators of landscape-scale forest spatial patterns for reporting on biodiversity. The European Stakeholders Conference in Malahide (2004) adopted a pattern indicator called "connectivity/fragmentation of ecosystems" as one of 15 biodiversity headline indicators to report in describing progress towards convention for biological diversity targets, and the European Environment Agency has working groups to implement these 15 indicators (EEA-SEBI2010 2006). Another international framework is the Montréal Process Criteria and Indicators (MPCI), which involves 12 countries with 90 percent of the world's temperate and boreal forests (MPLO 2000). The Montréal Process Working Group on Criteria and Indicators, formed in 1994, developed criteria and indicators for the conservation and sustainable management of forests, including indicators of forest fragmentation. The contributors to this report also produce other forest assessments that could be harmonized with these frameworks.

Metrics describing forest spatial patterns can be viewed as either direct or indirect indicators of forest biodiversity (fig. 1). The metrics are direct measures of biodiversity in the sense that biodiversity encompasses ecosystem diversity as well as genetic and species diversity (fig. 1B), and forest spatial pattern is an element of ecosystem diversity (e.g., MPLO 1995). From another perspective, the spatial pattern of forest land is an indirect indicator (fig. 1A) because it affects habitat quality for wildlife, which in turn affects the distribution and abundance of species and, ultimately, biodiversity. Spatial pattern is often characterized in terms of fragmentation (the disruption of continuity) and connectivity (the linkages that remain after fragmentation). As fragmentation proceeds, average fragment size and total fragment area decrease, and the insularity of fragments increases. Fragmentation increases the "edge effect" of the

[1] Kurt Riitters, USDA Forest Service, Southern Research Station, Research Triangle Park, NC 27709; and Christine Estreguil, European Commission - DG Joint Research Centre, Institute for Environment and Sustainability, Land Management and Natural Hazards Unit, Ispra, Italy.

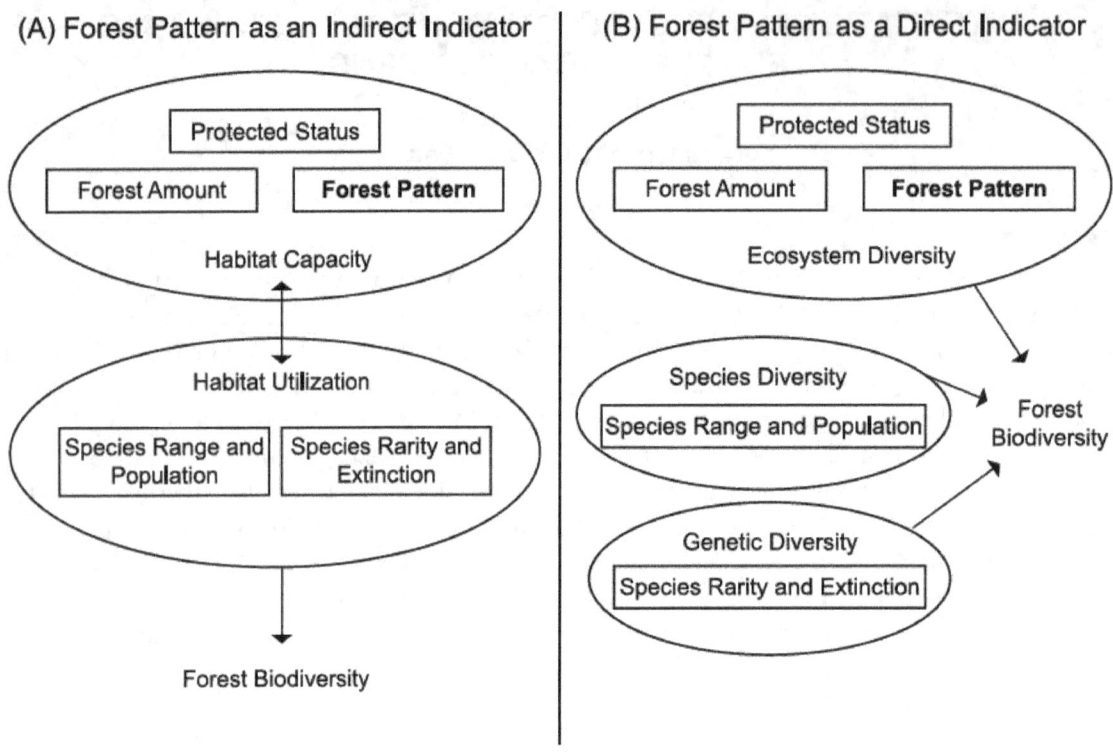

(A) Forest Pattern as an Indirect Indicator

Protected Status

Forest Amount | **Forest Pattern**

Habitat Capacity

Habitat Utilization

Species Range and Population | Species Rarity and Extinction

Forest Biodiversity

(B) Forest Pattern as a Direct Indicator

Protected Status

Forest Amount | **Forest Pattern**

Ecosystem Diversity

Species Diversity

Species Range and Population

Genetic Diversity

Species Rarity and Extinction

Forest Biodiversity

Figure 1—Forest pattern can be viewed as an (A) indirect or (B) direct indicator of biodiversity. As an indirect indicator, it describes habitat capacity and potential biodiversity. As a direct indicator, it describes the diversity of ecosystems as a component of biodiversity.

remaining forest, and it reduces the capability of organisms to move from one forested location to another. With fragmentation, plant and animal populations are more likely to become isolated, and the risk of extinction increases. Spatial pattern information addressing fragmentation and connectivity can provide spatially explicit indications of potentially dangerous changes for certain species. With this rationale, spatial pattern metrics describe habitat capacity and, thus, potential biodiversity.

International biodiversity assessments depend on consistency of measurements over large areas and typically employ a "top-down" approach. Forest area assessments can usually be accomplished by aggregating country-level estimates from ground-based inventories (e.g., FAO 2005), but aggregation of forest pattern estimates is usually not feasible because current field measurements of fragmentation (e.g., distance to the nearest forest edge) are only evolving in forest inventories. Forest maps are needed to measure forest spatial patterns, but maps for different countries rarely are consistent with each other. Differences in spatial resolution, nomenclature, and other map characteristics prevent aggregation of measurements. This has led to a reliance on remote sensing (satellite imagery) to provide consistent forest maps for assessments. Satellite technology makes it possible to conduct assessments, but the forest maps based on it lack many details. This trade-off leads to an emphasis on "top-down" assessments (i.e., coarse-scale assessment followed by in-depth study where needed) and on measurement procedures that can be implemented and interpreted at multiple spatial scales.

THE NEED FOR A RESEARCH SYMPOSIUM

Although land-cover maps derived from satellite imagery have been available for many years, they are available for only a few intensively studied places. Globally consistent maps are relatively new, and the first global assessment of forest fragmentation based on those maps was produced only 5 years ago. Also, during the last 5 years, the first national-level assessments have been conducted using even more detailed land-cover maps from satellite imagery in many countries (e.g., Australian Government 2003, New Zealand Ministry of Agriculture and Forestry 2003, USDA Forest Service 2004). In Europe, there is a need to harmonize national forest inventories (NFI) in terms of definitions and assessment protocols, and forest fragmentation is not systematically included within the national level programs. One goal is to improve the quality of European forest resource and forest environment data and the ability of the NFIs to meet both European and international reporting requirements (COST 2006). Forest fragmentation is currently addressed within research programs, and forest spatial pattern will be included for European-level reporting in the next MCPFE report, which is to be issued in 2007. As is expected in the application of a new technology, these initial experiences have suggested additional research and prompted discussion of changes to assessment protocols. These are matters of discussion among participants and stakeholders in international assessment groups, and our purpose in convening the symposium was to help inform those discussions.

The three papers in the symposium were drawn from six contributors to provide a range of perspectives from assessment specialists who have reported on forest spatial patterns in relation to biodiversity at national and international scales. By conducting assessments or research in support of those assessments, the contributors to the symposium have identified key research problems that require solutions in order to improve future assessments. Research problems related to the spatial scale, accuracy, and repeatability of mapping forest from satellite imagery, the selection of appropriate quantitative indices to use with the maps, the specification of reporting (aggregation) units, and the interpretation of spatial pattern statistics with respect to habitat quality and species diversity are identified in the papers. As the nations of the world proceed towards greater harmonization of forest assessment protocols to inform policy and management discussions, it is our expectation that many research issues identified by this report will be solved, resulting in improved biodiversity assessments at national and international scales.

LITERATURE CITED

Australian Government. 2003. Australia's state of the forests report. Canberra ACT: Bureau of Rural Sciences. http://www.brs. gov.au/stateoftheforests/. [Date accessed: April 24, 2006].

COST. 2006. E43 Harmonisation of national forest inventories in Europe: techniques for common reporting. http://www.metla.fi/ eu/cost/e43/. [Date accessed: April 24, 2006].

EEA-SEBI2010. 2006. Streamlining European 2010 biodiversity indicators. http://biodiversity-chm.eea.eu.int/information/ indicator/F1090245995/. [Date accessed: April 24, 2006].

FAO [Food and Agriculture Organization of the United Nations]. 2005. Global forest resources assessment 2005. Rome: FAO For. Pap. 147. http://www.fao.org/forestry/index.jsp. [Date accessed: April 24, 2006].

MCPFE [Ministerial Conference on the Protection of Forests in Europe]. 2005. MCPFE work programme: Pan-European follow-up of the fourth ministerial conference on the protection of forests in Europe. Warsaw, Poland: ministerial conference on the protection of forests in Europe, Liaison Unit Warsaw, ul. Bitwy Warszawskiej 1920 r. nr 3, 00-973. http://www.mcpfe.org/ publications. [Date accessed: April 24, 2006].

MPLO [Montréal Process Liaison Office]. 1995. Criteria and indicators for the conservation and sustainable management of temperate and boreal forests (Santiago Declaration). Ottawa, Canada: The Montréal Process Liaison Office, Canadian Forest Service. http://www.mpci.org/rep-pub/1995/santiagoe html. [Date accessed: April 24, 2006].

MPLO [Montréal Process Liaison Office]. 2000. Montréal process year 2000 progress report – progress and innovation in implementing criteria and indicators for the conservation and sustainable management of temperate and boreal forests. Ottawa, Canada. The Montréal Process Liaison Office, Canadian Forest Service. http://www.mpci.org/rep-pub/2000/rep2000e html. [Date accessed: April 24, 2006].

New Zealand Ministry of Agriculture and Forestry. 2003. Montréal country rep. 2003. 156 p. http://www.maf.govt.nz/forestry/ montreal-process/nz-country-rpt-2003.pdf. [Date accessed: April 24, 2006].

USDA Forest Service. 2004. National report on sustainable forests – 2003. FS-766. Washington, DC: USDA Forest Service. 139 p. http://www fs fed.us/research/sustain/documents/SustainableForests.pdf. [Date accessed: April 24, 2006].

FOREST FRAGMENTATION RESEARCH IDENTIFIED BY THE U.S. 2003 NATIONAL ASSESSMENT FOR THE MONTRÉAL PROCESS

Kurt Riitters[1]

Abstract—"Fragmentation of forest types" is an indicator of biological diversity in the Montréal Process. In the 2003 U.S. National Assessment, the indicator was interpreted as the extent to which forests are distributed as large blocks of habitat. It was assessed by measuring patch size, amount of edge, interpatch distance, and patch contrast on land-cover maps derived from satellite imagery. Although the available data permitted a good characterization of the four metrics at continental scale, it is too early to prove the relationships between those metrics and actual biological diversity. Instead, attention should be focused on improving the conceptual model that links forest spatial patterns to biological diversity and on testing alternate metrics in that framework.

INTRODUCTION

The Montréal Process is a framework for reporting forest sustainability indicators for 12 countries comprising 90 percent of the world's temperate and boreal forest area (MPLO 1995). The framework includes nine criteria addressing a variety of concerns that society has about forests and 67 indicators that measure specific aspects of those criteria. Nine indicators of genetic, species, and ecosystem diversity address the biodiversity criterion, and fragmentation of forest types is one of the indicators of ecosystem diversity. The United States is committed to periodic reporting of these indicators for the Montréal Process, and the U.S. 2003 National Report on Sustainable Forests (Darr 2004, USDA Forest Service 2004) is the first full report. The implementation of the fragmentation indicator for the U.S. 2003 report is reviewed in this paper with a view towards discussion of alternatives and recommendations to improve future reports.

Together with the Sustainable Forest Data Working Group of the Federal Geographic Data Committee, the Roundtable on Sustainable Forests convened public and expert workshops to reach agreement on how to evaluate sustainability (USDA Forest Service 2004). The Roundtable evaluated the data and information requirements for assessing forest fragmentation and made recommendations that were the point of departure for the research described in this paper. The group recommended data sources, metrics of fragmentation, and a reporting framework (table 1). The conceptual model focused on the characteristics of unbroken or intact forest land and viewed fragmentation as a measure of habitat quality and, thus, as an indirect measure of biodiversity. The Roundtable recognized many limitations to the recommended approach including:

- The approach describes forest fragmentation, not forest-type fragmentation.
- The metrics do not recognize movement corridors.
- The approach does not distinguish natural from anthropogenic fragmentation.
- The interpretation depends on the context to understand the implication of observed fragmentation.
- There are no standards or baselines for comparisons.

[1] USDA Forest Service, Southern Research Station, Research Triangle Park, NC 27709.

Table 1—Recommended forest fragmentation assessment protocols from the roundtable on sustainable forests as implemented in the 2003 United States report[a]

Assessment protocol	Recommendations as implemented in the United States report
Data source	1992 land-cover map for the conterminous 48 States, derived from Thematic Mapper Satellite Imagery with a spatial resolution of 0.09 ha/pixel and a thematic resolution of forest and nonforest.
Fragmentation metrics	Area-weighted average forest patch size, average minimum distance between forest patches, average forest patch contrast, average amount of forest edge per unit of forest area. (Patch contrast refers to the physiognomic difference between forest patches and adjacent nonforest patches.)
Reporting framework	Measurements of fragmentation metrics made within a grid of non-overlapping 56.25 km² (7.5 km x 7.5 km) analysis units, and aggregated into four large geographic regions (North, South, Pacific Northwest, and Rocky Mountain).

[a] Additional details are provided by Riitters and others (2004).

RESULTS

The following is a brief summary of results that have been previously reported elsewhere (Riitters and others 2004, Darr 2004). The term "landscape" is used in the following discussion to refer to a fixed-area, a 56.25 km² analysis unit (see table 1).

Patch Contrast

Landscapes with low patch contrast are generally forest-dominated, whereas high contrast landscapes contain small amounts of forest embedded in agricultural or urban lands. Landscapes with intermediate patch contrast contain intermediate amounts of forest in combination with agriculture or urban land uses or both. Patch contrast tends to be very high or very low in the North, South, and Pacific Northwest and intermediate in the Rocky Mountain region (table 2). When the gross distribution of forest is considered (this is not shown in table 2), the results indicate that 70 percent of all forest is contained in the one-third of landscapes that is forest dominated, 15 percent is contained in the one-third of landscapes with intermediate patch contrast, and the remaining 15 percent of forest is contained in the one-third of landscapes with high patch contrast.

Weighted Average Patch Size and Forest Edge per Unit Forest Area

The results for these two metrics are presented together because they are highly correlated with each other ($r = -0.69$) and with the amount of forest present in a given landscape ($r = 0.94$ and -0.82). In landscapes containing a large amount of forest, the average patch size is large, and the amount of forest edge is low. Where there is less forest area, the average patch size is smaller, and the amount of forest edge is larger. Because of these correlations, the maps of metric values either mimic or mirror the map of forest area (fig. 1). The analysis of forest edge shows that typical landscapes contain 10 to 40 percent of the maximum amount of edge they could contain for the amount of forest present, and that over-dispersed patterns (e.g., checkerboard) rarely span entire landscapes. The analysis of forest patch sizes, after adjusting for the amount of forest present, suggests that a given amount of forest tends to be arranged either as compactly as possible (large average patch size), or as dispersed as possible (small average patch size).

Distance between Forest Patches

The average distance between forest patches was also sensitive to the amount of forest present and exhibited very little variation (fig. 1). In landscapes containing less than 5-percent forest, the perimeter of a typical forest patch is 200 to 300 m from its nearest neighbor. In landscapes containing more than 5-percent forest, that distance is approximately 100 m.

Table 2—Patch contrast by geographic region

Geographic region	Number of analysis units with forest	Contrast score						
		Low contrast 1.0	1.5	2.0	Medium contrast 2.5	3.0	3.5	High contrast 4.0
		- - - - - - - - - - - *percent of analysis units in region* - - - - - - - - - - -						
North	30,260	43.2	0.0	0.0	0.5	0.0	0.0	56.3
South	36,635	50.0	0.3	11.7	2.0	4.9	1.5	29.5
Pacific Coast	13,970	41.1	2.2	32.5	1.5	6.4	0.5	15.8
Rocky Mountain	46,147	16.6	1.3	31.1	1.4	26.8	1.5	21.2
All regions	127,012	35.3	0.8	18.3	1.4	11.9	1.0	31.4

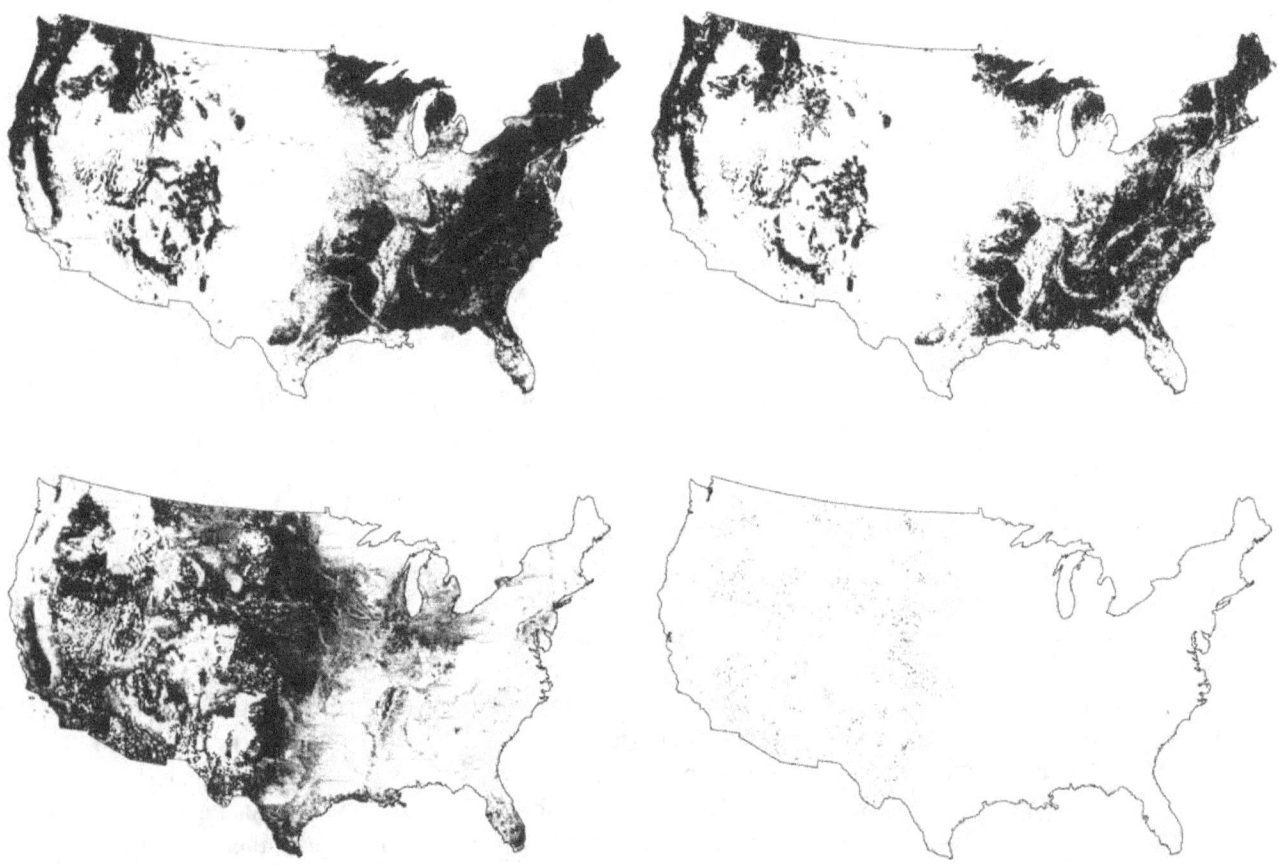

Figure 1—Maps of fragmentation metrics in the U.S. 2003 Montréal Process Report. The maps are shaded from low (light) to high (dark) according to the value of the metric within a 7.5- by 7.5- km analysis unit. Clockwise from top left: percent forest area, weighted average forest patch size, average minimum distance between forest patches, and amount of forest edge-per-unit forest area.

DISCUSSION

The United States implementation of the fragmentation indicator was considered to be experimental because the Roundtable recommendations had never before been implemented over such a large area with satellite-based, land cover maps. The most striking finding from the implementation was that if the amount of forest is known, then three of the four recommended metrics provided little additional information regarding forest fragmentation. The fourth metric patch contrast added information about the landscape context of forest that could not be predicted from the amount of forest alone.

The motivating question for the IUFRO symposium was about the research needed to improve future implementations of the forest fragmentation indicator. Three of the five recognized limitations of the implementation (listed earlier in this paper) refer to inability to interpret the results. This suggests that research should focus on the pattern-process hypothesis, that is, on understanding the implications of observed fragmentation. Whereas such research is important, it may be premature because the recommended metrics are not even different (statistically) from each other and sometimes are not different from a simple metric of forest amount. In other words, improved interpretative ability will not help if the metrics cannot distinguish between forest amount and forest spatial pattern or distinguish among different types and degrees of forest fragmentation. At the same time, the recommended metrics might be more interpretable if only more detailed maps were available. This suggests that research should focus on producing more detailed forest maps for future analyses. However, as a practical matter, national land cover maps are very expensive to produce, and the new maps (MRLC 2006) that will be used for the next Montréal Process assessment are similar to the maps used in the present study.

One way to identify research starts by stipulating the available data because it makes little sense to recommend any assessment approach that cannot be implemented. The research goal is then to choose metrics and a reporting framework that make the best use of the available data. This perspective identifies a change in the conceptual model as the most important research question. The Roundtable used conceptual models based on theory from island biogeography (MacArthur and Wilson 1967) and metapopulation ecology (e.g., Hanski 1999), both of which employ forest "patches" as a basic landscape element, so that recommended metrics included patch-based metrics such as patch size, distance between patches, and patch contrast. But, when the best available data are used, the results show that the very concept of forest patches only applies to, at most, 30 percent of all forest. The conceptual model is too fine-scaled and detailed for the available data.

Hierarchy theory (O'Neill and others 1986) and complexity theory (see Milne 1998) might be considered as theoretical frameworks. According to hierarchy theory, forest fragmentation could be viewed as a constraining property of landscapes that contain forests as opposed to a mechanistic driver of biodiversity within landscapes. Suitable metrics would address larger scale questions such as how much forest exists in patchy landscapes, as opposed to finer scale questions such as how patch size affects biodiversity. This approach would identify the landscapes where physical fragmentation was a concern, and, in these places, it would be worthwhile to use the previously recommended patch-based metrics in follow-up studies. Complexity theory focuses on long-term dynamics and the likelihood that entire landscapes will undergo "phase changes" in forest fragmentation that could signal imminent and profound changes in biodiversity. For example, it would be very informative to know that a given landscape is near a threshold between a forest-dominated landscape and a patchy forest landscape because an interpretation with respect to biodiversity can be made even if all of the detailed species-specific responses cannot be predicted. Complexity theory is usually cast in the temporal domain and typically requires a long time series of information for analysis, but it still might be possible to examine questions of vulnerability to phase changes in the next Montréal Process report.

CONCLUSION

A review of the U.S. implementation of the fragmentation indicator in the first Montréal Process report identified a key research question that should be addressed in preparation for the next Montréal Process report. It is recommended that the process start with realistic assumptions about the best available data, and, on that basis, the most important research is to revise the conceptual model and associated fragmentation metrics. The collection of more detailed data or an investment in research to improve the interpretation of existing coarse-scale data or both is less likely to lead to improvements in future reports.

LITERATURE CITED

Darr, D., coord. 2004. Data report: A supplement to the national report on sustainable forests—2003. FS-766A. Washington, DC: USDA Forest Service. http://www fs fed.us/research/sustain/contents.htm. [Date accessed: April 24, 2006].

Hanski, I. 1999. Metapopulation ecology. Oxford, UK: Oxford University Press. 324 p.

MacArthur, R.H.; Wilson, E.O. 1967. The theory of island biogeography. Princeton, NJ: Princeton University Press. 224 p.

Milne, B.T. 1998. Motivations and benefits of complex system approaches in ecology. Ecosystems. 1: 449-456.

MPLO [Montréal Process Liaison Office]. 1995. Criteria and indicators for the conservation and sustainable management of temperate and boreal forests (Santiago Declaration). Ottawa, Canada: The Montréal Process Liaison Office, Canadian Forest Service. http://www mpci.org/rep-pub/1995/santiagoe html. [Date accessed: April 24, 2006].

MRLC [Multi-Resolution Land Characteristics]. 2006. The MRLC consortium. http://www mrlc.gov/. [Date accessed: April 24, 2006].

O'Neill, R.V.; DeAngelis, D.L.; Waide, J.B.; Allen, T.H.F. 1986. A hierarchical concept of ecosystems. Princeton, NJ: Princeton University Press. 262 p.

Riitters, K.H.; Wickham, J.D.; Coulston, J.W. 2004. A preliminary assessment of Montréal Process indicators of forest fragmentation for the United States. Environmental Monitoring and Assessment. 91: 257-276.

USDA Forest Service. 2004. National report on sustainable forests—2003. FS-766. Washington, DC: USDA Forest Service. 139 p. http://www fs fed.us/research/sustain/. [Date accessed: April 24, 2006].

MONTRÉAL PROCESS REPORTING ON FOREST FRAGMENTATION IN NEW ZEALAND—CURRENT STATUS AND RESEARCH

Thomas Paul, Barbara Hock, and Tim Payn[1]

Abstract—The indicator value of forest fragmentation for biological diversity in the Montréal Process is highly dependent on the quality of the underlying data, the characteristics of metrics used to describe the fragmentation, and the appropriate use of both in the chosen context. In the first stage and for the production of the 2003 New Zealand report on the Montréal Process, only the size-class distribution of indigenous forests was used as a measure for fragmentation of forests. The current research on delivering a more accurate picture about the fragmentation of forests in New Zealand is described. It is based on new datasets on the occurrence of indigenous and plantation forests at a national scale. The usability and quality of these datasets for forest fragmentation evaluation is described, and issues are highlighted. A number of indices and metrics were investigated for their ability to describe forest fragmentation at two legislation-based scales—the national and the regional level. The results, recommendations, and further research needs are described.

INTRODUCTION

New Zealand is a member of the Montréal Process Criteria and Indicator Working Group established in 1993. The purpose of this group is to develop a set of criteria and indicators for assessing the management of temperate and boreal forests in terms of sustainability and the progress toward sustainable management. In New Zealand's first country report in 2003, a first attempt was made to assess and report on the country's progress toward sustainable forest management at the national level (Ministry of Agriculture and Forestry 2002). The report includes only a small number of indicators and the reporting on Criterion 1—Conservation of Biological Diversity. Fragmentation of forest types dealt only with the patch sizes of the indigenous forest as a measure of fragmentation at the national level (Ministry of Agriculture and Forestry 2002). With increasing software capability and as more detailed national information becomes available, the implementation and use of other indicators on fragmentation becomes possible.

A problem arising when dealing with fragmentation is the high and still increasing amount of metrics that can be used to quantify fragmentation or certain aspects of it (McGarigal and Marks 1994). Harris (1984) defines fragmentation as a landscape-level process in which patches are progressively subdivided into smaller, geometrically more complex and more isolated fragments as a result of both natural processes and human land use activities. In addition, one single metric is not capable of capturing the entire complexity of fragmentation (Cain and others 1997). In order to understand underlying trends, different aspects of the fragmentation process have to be captured and represented (Neel and others 2004). When selecting appropriate metrics, it is also obviously important to avoid sets of metrics that have a high correlation with each other (Cushman and others, in press).

In the following sections, we present results on forest fragmentation under the Montréal reporting Criterion for the Conservation of Biological Diversity and ways to measure and describe the status of fragmentation in New Zealand. The basic metrics that we used for this assessment of the status of fragmentation research and development in New Zealand are the percentage of forest, the mean patch size, and the patch number, as they are easily understandable and less complex than other metrics.

In order to assess progress to more sustainable forest management, it is necessary to be able to compare the status of the forest at different points in time. This requires the ability to compare current datasets with those used previously.

---

[1] Thomas Paul, Barbara Hock, and Tim Payn, ENSIS Environment, Te Papa Tipu Innovation Park, Rotorua, New Zealand.

In the first part, problems and possible difficulties that could arise when using different datasets are shown. In the second part, the change of fragmentation in New Zealand between 1996 and 2001 at the national and regional level is presented based on the metrics listed above. Issues with using the chosen metrics at different scales are discussed.

New Zealand has a total land area of around 27 million ha spread over two major islands and a number of smaller islands. At the time of the first Montréal report in 2003, approximately 8.1 million ha of land were covered with forest (Ministry of Agriculture and Forestry 2003). Of the 30 percent of New Zealand's total land area covered by forests, the dominant forest type was indigenous forests (23 percent). Seven percent was covered with planted forests represented mainly by monospecies *Pinus radiata* D. Don plantations. These two types of forest estates differ in terms of ownership, management, and objectives with almost all of the indigenous forests forming part of the country's conservation estate and, hence, protected from harvesting. Differences in biological characteristics exist, but the importance of plantation forests for biodiversity and other environmental benefits has been often overlooked in New Zealand when assessing forest values at the landscape level (Brockerhoff and others 2001).

MATERIAL AND METHODS
We used the New Zealand Land Cover Database (LCDB) Versions 1 and 2 as the information source for the location of forests in New Zealand (Thompson and others 2003). Version 1 represents the status of land cover in summer 1996/1997, whereas Version 2 represents the status in the summer of 2000/2001. LCDB 1 is based on SPOT images with a 30-m resolution and a Minimum Mapping Unit of 1 ha (Miri 2004). The surface of New Zealand was classified into 18 land cover classes including inland water surfaces. LCDB 2 is based on Landsat 7 ETM+ images with a resolution of 15 m. The same minimum mapping unit of 1 ha was applied, but, in certain circumstances, submapping was possible (Miri 2004). A more detailed classification was used consisting of 43 land cover classes that were hierarchically based on the former classes of LCDB 1 (table 1, first two columns).

As a result of the changes in processing and delineation of the satellite data for LCDB 2, a more precise picture of the land cover of New Zealand was drawn. In order to also improve the precision of LCDB 1, this database was revisited, and a revised version of LCDB 1 was included with the new classification, referred to in this paper as LCDB 1 v2.

The revision of the LCDB 1 was carried out with additional and improved data such as aerial photography, additional spatial databases, and a higher standard of manual checking that increased the delineation accuracy. Previous problems with the very similar signatures of planted forests and broadleaved indigenous hardwoods could also be resolved (Miri 2004), (Personal communication. 2005. S. Murray. Terralink International Limited, 275 Cuba Street, Wellington 6011, New Zealand).

The two LCDB 1 datasets enabled us to compare two processing and delineation procedures and their impact on the reporting on forest fragmentation based on these two versions of New Zealand's land cover. Using the revised and improved LCDB 1 and LCDB 2, we were able to compare the land cover status of 1996 with the situation in 2000/2001 and track changes over that period of time with a reasonable degree of accuracy.

To focus on forest fragmentation and its change, we needed to combine land cover classes that are considered to be forests. However, we still distinguished between indigenous forests and plantation forests because of their very different legal status and nature. In the indigenous forest class that we used for the Montréal Process analysis, we included the land cover classes indigenous forests, manuka and kanuka, and hardwoods. Whereas manuka and kanuka are also considered to be scrubs, we included this class because of its often forest-like structure growing to a maximum height of 8 to 10 m (kanuka) or 2 to 6 m (manuka) with the lower heights usually on very dry South Island sites. The hardwoods class (also

Table 1—Classes of LCDB 1 and LCDB 2 and composite classes for the study

LCDB 1 class	LCDB 2 class	Compiled to this class for this study
Urban area	Built up area	Urban
Urban open space	Urban parkland/open space	Urban
Mines and dumps	Surface mine Dump Transport infrastructure	Others
Coastal sand	Coastal sand and gravel	
Bare ground	River and lakeshore gravel and rock Landslide Alpine gravel and rock Permanent snow and ice Alpine grass-/herbfield	
Inland water	Lake and pond River Estuarine open water	
Primarily horticulture	Short-rotation cropland Vineyard Orchard and other perennial crops	
Primarily pastoral	High producing exotic grassland Low producing grassland	Production grasslands
Tussock grassland	Tall tussock grassland Depleted grassland	
Inland wetland	Herbaceous freshwater vegetation	Others
Coastal wetland	Herbaceous saline vegetation Flaxland	
Scrub	Fernland Gorse and/or broom Manuka and/or kanuka Matagouri Broadleaved indigenous hardwoods Sub alpine shrubland Mixed exotic shrubland Grey scrub	Scrubland Scrubland Indigenous forest Scrubland Indigenous forest Scrubland Scrubland Scrubland
Major shelterbelts	Minor shelterbelts (not recognized in LCDB 1) Major shelterbelts	Others
Planted forest	Afforestation (not imaged) Afforestation (imaged, post LCDB 1) Forest - harvested Pine forest—open canopy Pine forest—closed canopy Other exotic forest	Planted forest
Willows and poplars	Deciduous hardwoods	Others[a]
Indigenous forest	Indigenous forest Mangrove	Indigenous forest Others

[a] The structure of this class excludes it from the forest class for Montréal reporting as it typically consists of narrow plantings such as riparian buffers.

called Broadleaved Indigenous Hardwoods) is similarly forest-like with canopy heights in the 3- to 7-m range. Both the manuka and kanuka and hardwoods classes usually represent an advanced successional stage back to indigenous forest (Thompson and others 2003), (Personal communication. 2005. B. Burns, Scientist. Landcare Research, Private Bag 3127, Hamilton, New Zealand). For the plantation forest class that we used for Montréal reporting we collated all stages of pine and exotic tree plantations. This includes harvested and newly replanted areas, assuming that as a result of the fast growth of exotic trees, these areas will show a forest structure in a relatively short period of time. The remaining classes of LCDB 1 and 2 were grouped into scrubland, urban, production grasslands, cropland, and other (table 1).

We used two methods to analyze the datasets. The first step was to calculate the frequency of forest patch sizes as a national scale measure similar to the approach used in the first Montréal report. This analysis and the additional calculations of the total area changes were carried out with ARCInfo 9.0 (ESRI 2004). The second step was a more detailed analysis of percentage area, mean patch size, and patch numbers as measures of fragmentation. These were calculated using Fragstats 3.3 (McGarigal and others 2002). This type of analysis required the conversion of the vector/polygon-based land cover database into raster format datasets. Because of limitations in computer memory, we split the whole dataset of LCDB 1 and 2 into the 16 administrative regions of New Zealand (table 2). As the regional authorities have jurisdiction over their regions, this approach retains legal authority-based reporting for the Montréal process report. We choose a raster size of 30 m for most of those regions. For six regions for which we exceeded the computable size, we had to choose a raster size of 60 m (table 2).

Table 2—Regions used for the calculation of metrics and their characteristics[a] (ordered from North to South)

	Region	Population	Total area of region (ha)	Land area used for farming in 2001 (ha)	Main occupational group
North Island	Northland[b]	~ 140,000	1 329 631	629 534	Agriculture and fishery
	Auckland	~ 1.5 Mio	432 078	258 715	Professionals
	Waikato	~ 357,000	2 684 337	1 317 284	Agriculture and fishery
	Bay of Plenty	~ 239,000	1 247 300	290 302	Service and sales
	Manuwatu - Wanganui (Horizon)[c]	~ 220,000	2 196 591	1 357 752	Service and sales
	Gisborne	~ 43,900	835 493	401 972	Agriculture and fishery
	Taranaki	~ 102,000	794 817	391 861	Agriculture and fishery
	Hawkes Bay	~ 143,000	1 276 983	769 704	Agriculture and fishery
	Greater Wellington	~ 423,000	805 564	396 885	Professionals
South Island	Marlborough	~ 39,500	1 249 347	461 558	Agriculture and fishery
	Nelson	~ 41,000	44 419	7 020	Service and sales
	Tasman	~ 41,000	977 498	193 307	Agriculture and fishery
	West Coast[b]	~ 30,000	2 335 146	364 590	Service and sales
	Canterbury[b]	~ 481,000	3 847 393	2 991 162	Service and sales
	Otago[b]	~ 181,000	3 628 442	2 362 393	Service and sales
	Southland[b]	~ 91,000	3 286 201	1 417 939	Agriculture and fishery

[a] Statistics New Zealand (2001).

[b] Regions were analysed with a 60-m raster instead of 30 m due to computing memory.

[c] For the Manuwatu–Wanganui region, the regional council name Horizon was used in diagrams.

RESULTS
Changes in Data Collection Methods

The comparison of the two land cover database versions for 1996 showed the differences between the two processing and delineation procedures. The differences that relate to forests and scrubland are shown in figure 1. The overall increase in forest area due to the different methods is clear. The indigenous forest area increased by 3.2 percent and planted forests by 13 percent. Part of this increase in forest area came from the reduction of scrubland area (-13 percent).

The qualitative nature of the LCDB 1 processing and the better quality of the process for LCDB 2 are reflected in the differences of the patch-size classes for indigenous forests (fig. 2). Differences occur

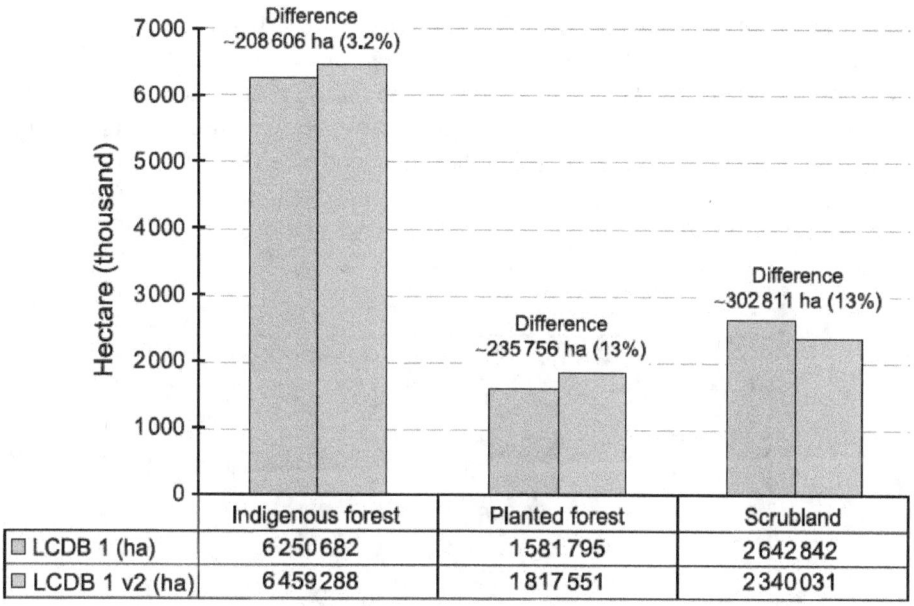

	Indigenous forest	Planted forest	Scrubland
☐ LCDB 1 (ha)	6 250 682	1 581 795	2 642 842
☐ LCDB 1 v2 (ha)	6 459 288	1 817 551	2 340 031

Figure 1—Land area differences of land cover classes as a result of different satellite imaginary and processing.

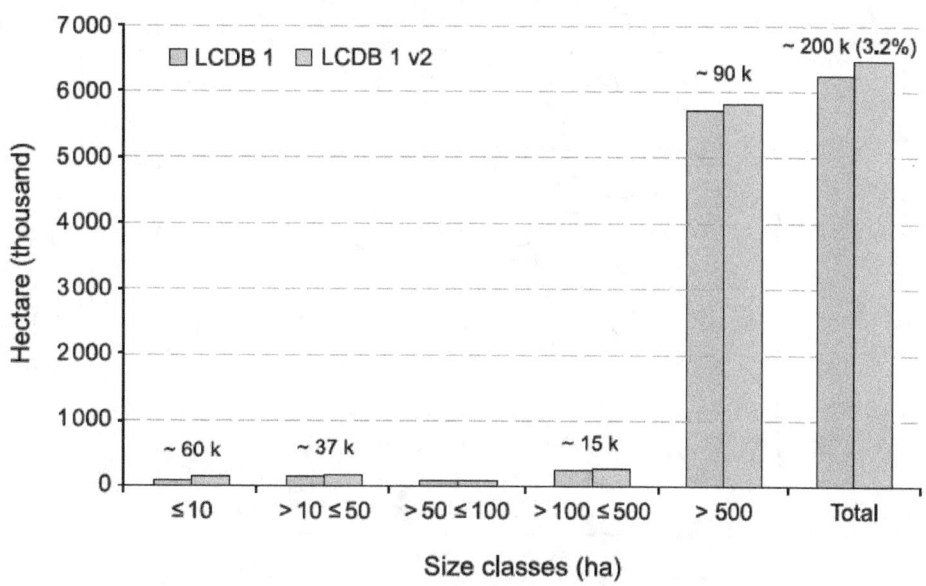

Figure 2—Differences in the total area of patch-size classes for indigenous forests due to two different processing methods and the use of additional datasets.

mainly for the smallest and largest patches. In patches smaller than 10 ha (60 000 ha difference) and between 10 and 50 ha (37 000 ha difference), nearly 50 percent of the total area differences occurred. The remaining 50 percent of area differences were found in patches over 500 ha. A comparison between both sets of indigenous forests showed that some of the changes in area in the higher size class were due to reclassification from scrub to indigenous forest. An example of the variability and differences between the two versions of LCDB 1 is given by figure 3. The example shown is the Mahia Peninsula at the eastern site of the North Island. The differences in the delineation and classification of the areas of indigenous forest are clearly visible.

Changes in Forested Land Area in New Zealand between 1996 and 2001
During the time period of the study, the total forest-land area increased by approximately 136 000 ha, or approximately 0.4 percent of the total land area. Planted forests (~ 139 000 ha) were nearly exclusively responsible for this increase in area, whereas indigenous forest areas in total changed slightly with a ~ 3500-ha loss mainly in the South Island (fig. 4). Most of the newly established planted forests occurred in the North Island. The conversion of ~ 120 000 ha of grassland used for farming (pasture) into planted forest was the greatest land area change between land uses (fig. 5). The conversion of indigenous forests and scrubland to planted forest was, by comparison, minor (~ 11 000 ha and ~ 8 000 ha, respectively). However, the major component of the decrease in indigenous forest cover was the

Figure 3—Mahia Peninsula. Differences in the indigenous forest cover due to different processing methods for the classification of land cover.

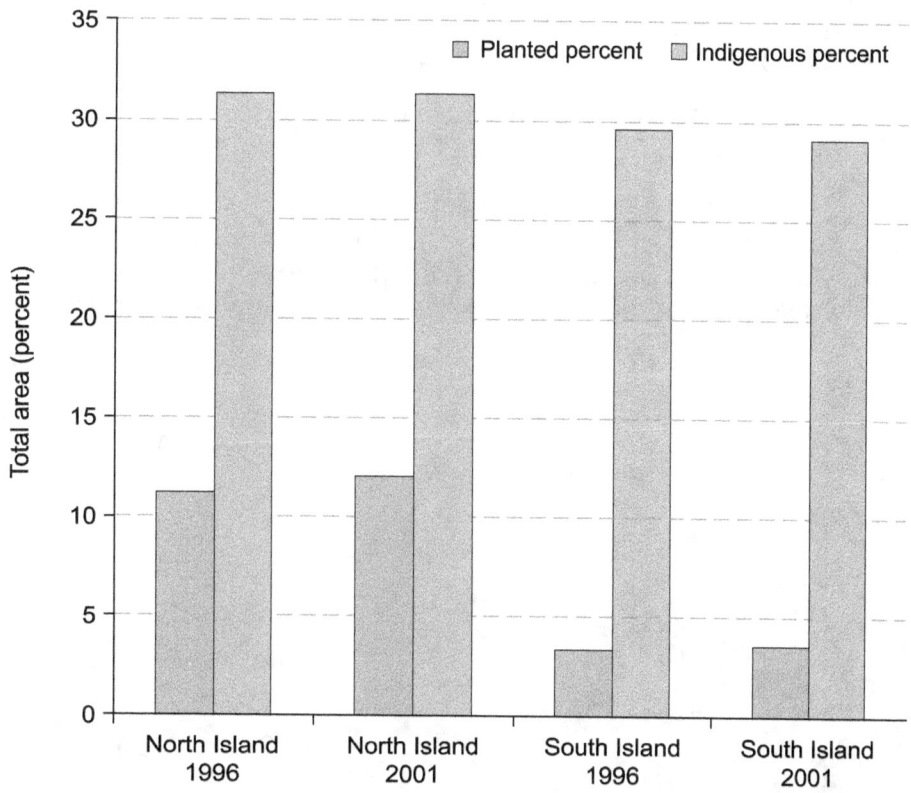

Figure 4—Percentage of total area covered by planted and indigenous forests for the two main islands of New Zealand for 1996 and 2001.

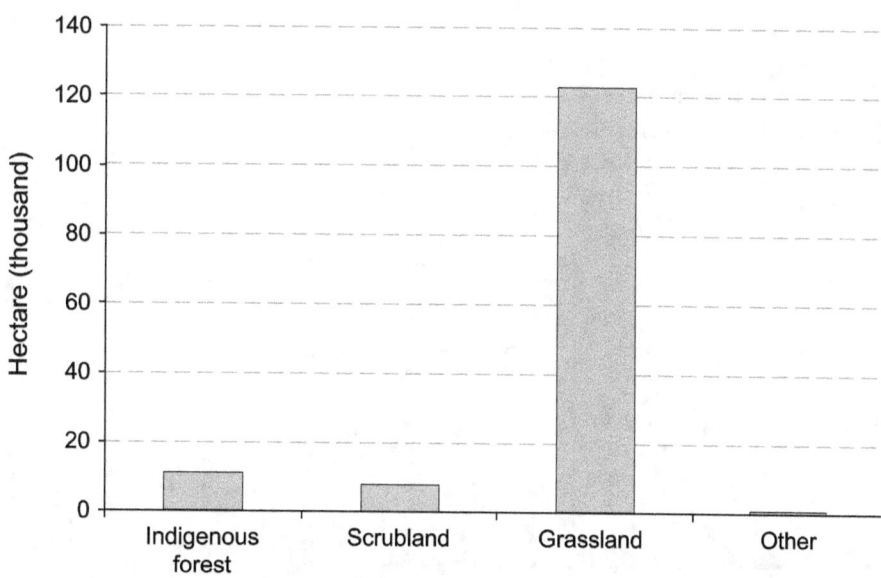

Figure 5—Area of indigenous forest, scrubland, grassland, and other land cover classes turned into planted forests between 1996 and 2001.

conversion of this forest type into planted forests. The conversion of indigenous forests to other land cover types was at a much smaller scale.

In contrast to the amount of land converted into planted forests, the loss of that type of forest to other land cover classes was negligible (fig. 6). The total planted forest losses were only 1400 ha compared to the total increase of ~ 141 000 ha.

Forest area changes at the regional level give an insight into the distribution of the losses and gains over the period (fig. 7). Minor decreases in indigenous forests occurred in the North Island regions of Gisborne and Wellington. On the South Island, the main decrease occurred in Marlborough where land

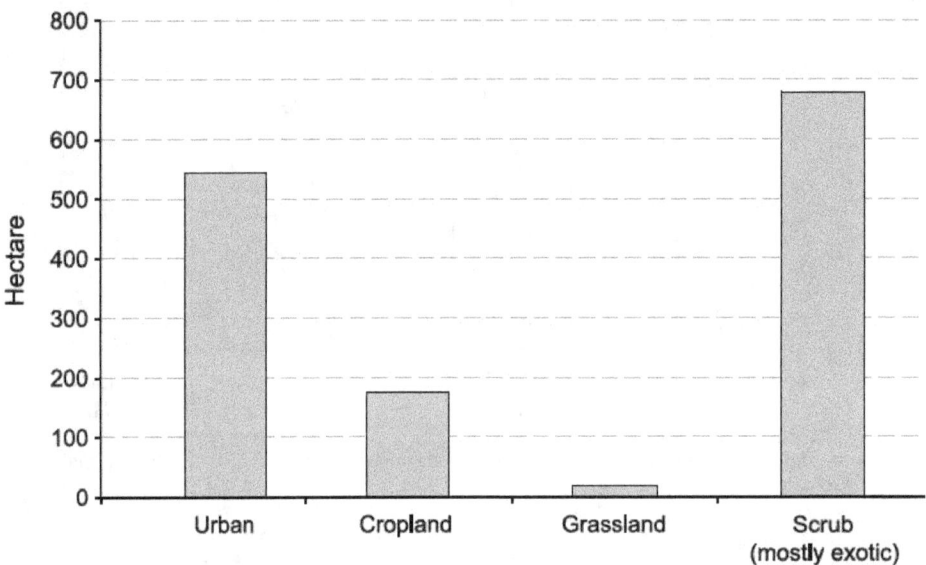

Figure 6—Area of planted forest turned into other land cover classes over the period between 1996 and 2001.

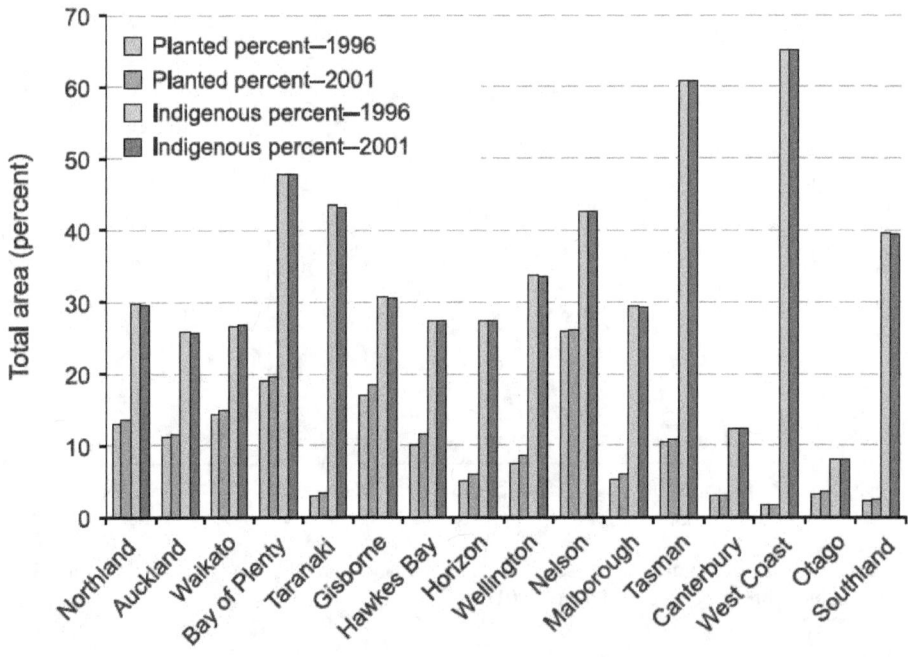

Figure 7—Changes in percent of the total area of planted and indigenous forest cover for the 16 regions of New Zealand between 1996 and 2001.

development and conversions into agricultural land cover reduced the indigenous forest cover markedly. Increases of planted forests occur in every region except Canterbury, where the area under planted forest cover remained constant. The highest increases occurred in the Gisborne and Wellington regions, which have already been mentioned for their decrease in indigenous forest cover. The greater increase of planted forests in the North Island can also be clearly seen at the regional level.

Patch Number and Size—Changes between 1996 and 2001

The small change in the total land area covered with indigenous forest is reiterated in the small change in the number in patch sizes for this forest type. The small changes in land area covered by indigenous forest didn't affect the size-class distribution at the national level (fig. 8). The increase of planted forest area was mainly due to an increase in the number of small-size plantations ranging from under 1 ha up to 100 ha. Over 4,600 patches of planted forests smaller than 100 ha were planted between 1996 and 2001.

A comparison of the number of indigenous forest patches by region showed no specific changes during the studied time period (fig. 9). The calculated mean patch size for the indigenous forests was also mostly constant for the regions (fig. 10). Small changes in the mean patch size occurred in five regions: Taranaki, Bay of Plenty, Wellington, Tasman, and Marlborough. The mean patch size decreased in these regions by around 0.5 to 1 ha over the 5 years. In other words, whereas the national size-class distribution remained the same for indigenous forests, the patch sizes within a class shrank slightly for these regions and were only detected on the regional level.

The national trend of increasing numbers of planted forests was obviously reflected at the regional level (fig. 11). The increase in the number of planted forest patches occurred with 3,937 new patches predominantly in the North Island regions. In the South Island, the increase in number of planted forests -was with 882 lower. Regions with already high forest cover like the West Coast did not show a strong increase in planted forest numbers.

The changes of mean patch size varied between the regions, but no definite trend was evident (fig. 12). The largest increases in the mean patch size occurred in Gisborne on the east coast of the North Island and in Marlborough on the South Island; those are areas with larger estates of planted forests. Comparing the mean patch size and the number of patches by region gives a picture of how new plantation forests

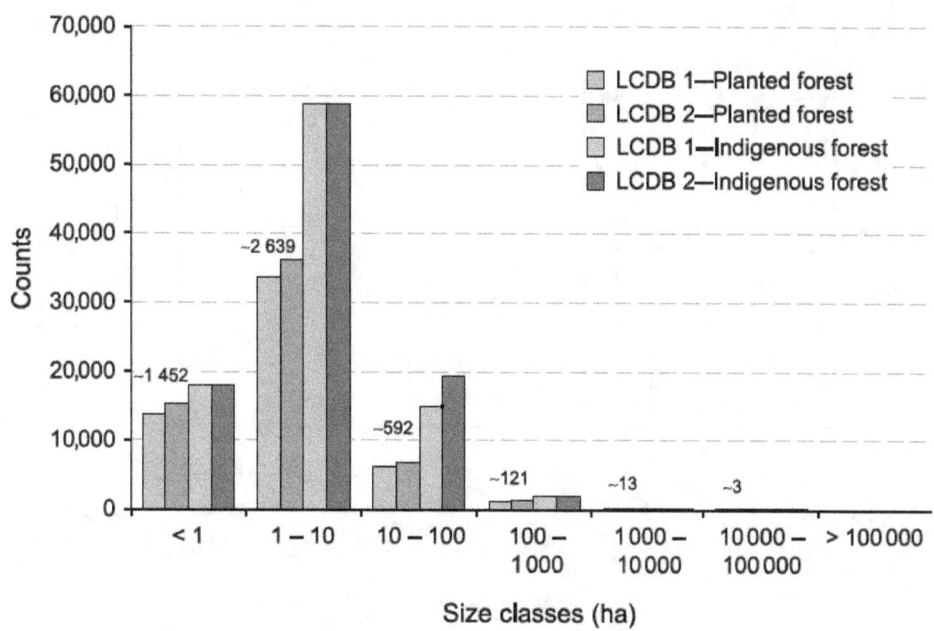

Figure 8—Patch size-class distribution and its change between 1996 and 2001 for the total forested area of New Zealand. Numbers above the bars show the amount of patches of planted forests that contributed to the increase in forested area.

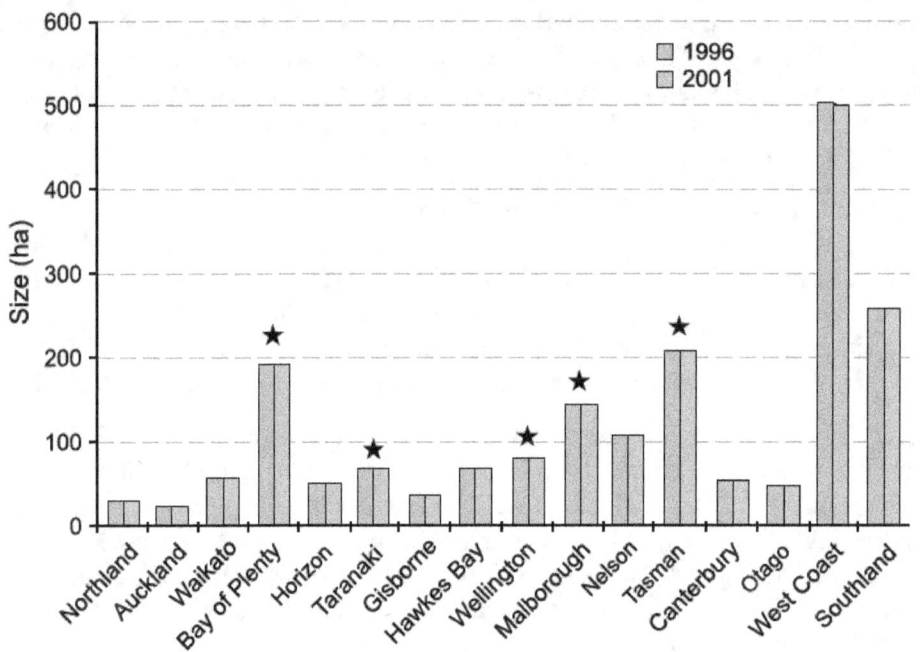

Figure 9—Comparison of mean patch sizes of indigenous forests by region. ★ = a small change of the mean patch size in five regions.

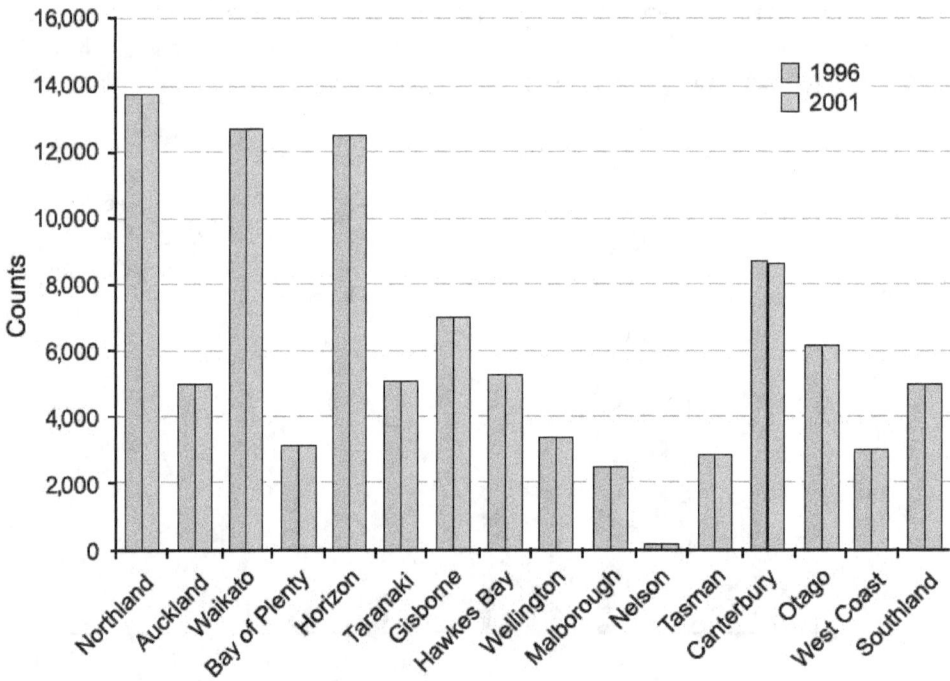

Figure 10—Comparison of number of indigenous forest patches by region.

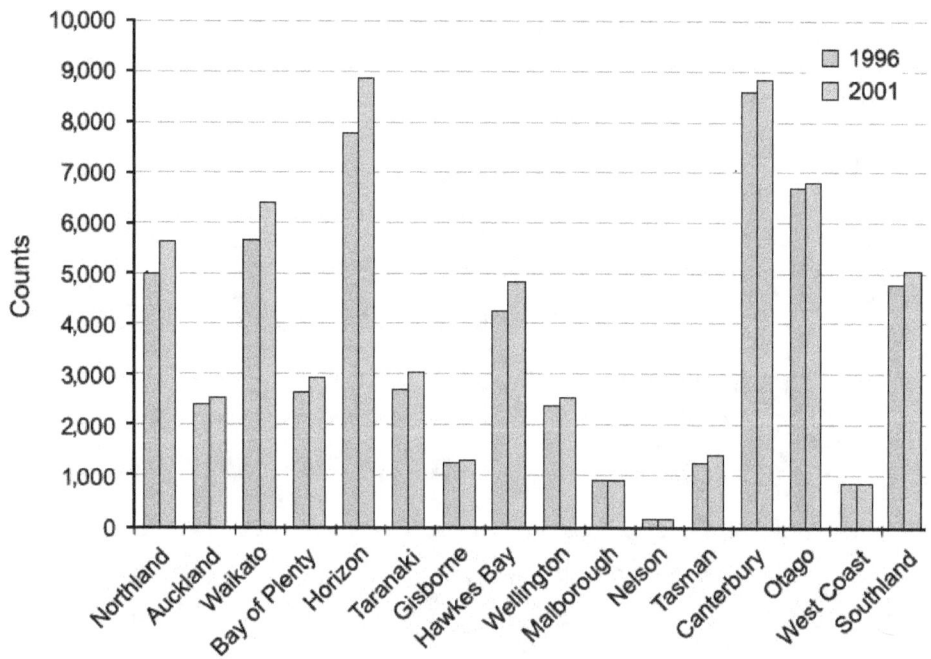

Figure 11—Comparison of number of planted forest patches by region.

were established. The increase in mean patch size, combined with no change in number of patches in the Gisborne region, indicates that the new forest plantings were often adjacent to existing ones. A similar trend occurred in Marlborough. By comparison, in the regions Manuwatu–Wanganui and Hawkes Bay, the number of patches increased, and the mean patch size stayed more or less the same, indicating new forests were planted separately from existing ones. In the regions Waikato, Bay of Plenty, Northland, and Tasman the mean patch size decreased, and the number of patches actually increased. This pattern could be the result of either small sized new plantations or increasing fragmentation of existing forests. The increase in the total area of planted forests in the regions indicates that at least, in part, the first scenario occurred.

Overall Picture of Forest Distribution–Status in 2001

The size distribution of indigenous forests and planted forests for the two Main Islands has been shown in figure 3. Whereas the distribution of indigenous forest between the islands is relatively balanced, the presence of planted forest is skewed toward the North Island.

Whereas indigenous forest is the predominant forest type in all 16 regions, the total percentage varies between the regions (fig. 13). Four of the six regions with the highest percentage of indigenous forests (over 35 percent of total land area) are located in the South Island, but this island also has the regions with the lowest indigenous forest cover, with the percentage of potential forest land being even less than 12 percent in 2001 (Otago and Canterbury). The West Coast, with over 60 percent of the total area under indigenous forest, has the highest percentage of this type of forest for all the regions. The Bay of Plenty region with 48 percent and the Taranaki region with 43 percent show the highest percentage of indigenous forest cover for the North Island. The percentage of indigenous forest for the other North Island regions is relatively evenly spread with values between 26 and 32 percent, whereas the South Island shows the highest variability between the regions in terms of indigenous forest cover.

Plantation forests show even more variation across the regions than the variable levels of indigenous forests. The percentage of plantations across the North Island regions is, on average with 11.3 percent in 2001, higher than for the South Island regions (average 6.4 percent). The lowest percentages occur in the Taranaki and Manuwatu–Wanganui regions (3.3 percent and 6 percent, respectively), and the

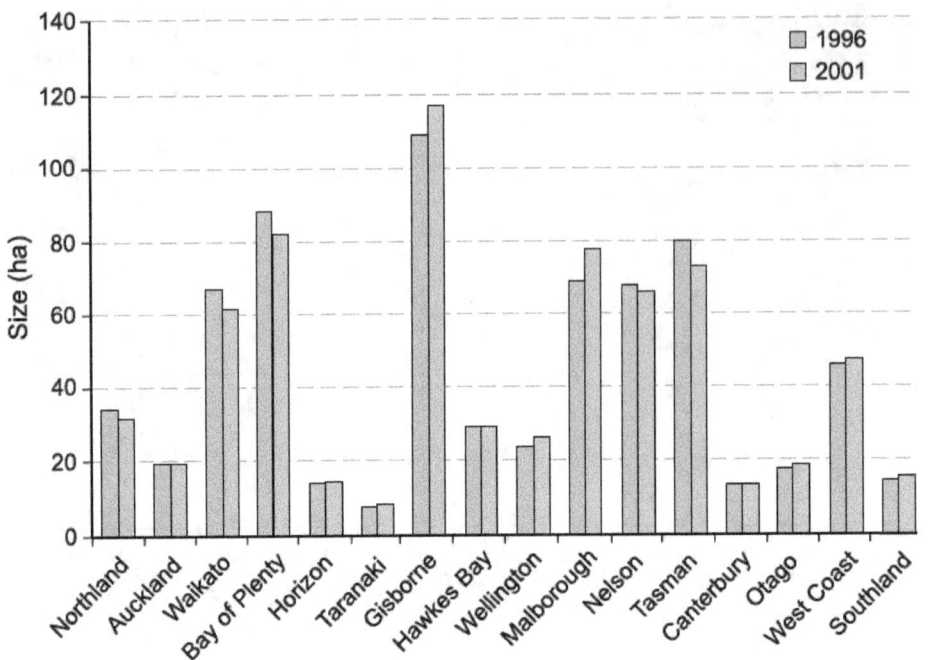

Figure 12—Comparison of mean patch size of planted forests by region.

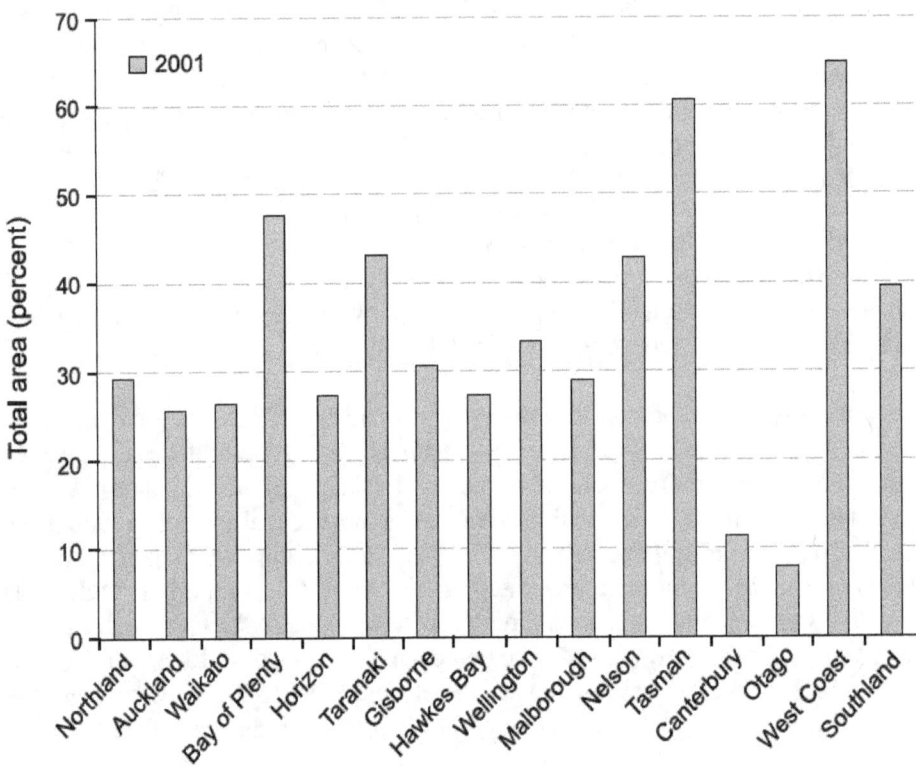

Figure 13—Percentage of total area covered by indigenous forests by region.

highest value of nearly 20 percent occurs for the Bay of Plenty region (fig. 14). The variability in the percentage of planted forest area is higher for the South Island regions than those in the North Island. The lowest values of planted forests are found in the regions with a high indigenous forest cover (Westland 1.8 percent and Southland 2.4 percent) and also in regions with a very low indigenous forest cover (Canterbury 2.9 percent and Otago 3.5 percent). Nelson is the exception in the South Island with a high percentage of indigenous forest (42 percent) as well as a high percentage of planted forest (25 percent).

In regions with a high percentage of indigenous forest cover, there is a tendency to higher mean patch sizes and lower number of patches. Westland, with an indigenous forest cover of 60 percent, consists of large unfragmented indigenous forest. The tendency of increasing patch size and reduced patch number is correlated to the proportion of area occupied by the relevant land cover class in the region. This means, with a high percentage of area occupied, the patch number decreases due to the problem of limited space to disperse smaller patches. However, for Westland, we believe that those results are an indication for low fragmentation because of the very low number of patches at a level of 60 percent cover. The Bay of Plenty, Tasman, and Southland region also follow this trend, even though the percentage of indigenous forests is less, and the mean patch size of around 200 ha is clearly smaller than the mean patch size of 500 ha on the West Coast.

In contrast to the above, regions with less than 30 percent indigenous cover have a high number of forest patches. Those regions have smaller, average-sized patches, typically less than 100 ha in size. Examples are Northland, Waikato, and Manuwatu–Wanganui for the North Island and Canterbury on the South Island. Those regions have a high percentage of land used for farming (table 2).

The Auckland region shows the effect of a high population on the forest fragmentation of a landscape. It has the smallest mean patch size and also a small number of patches. Other regions with large population centres like Christchurch (Canterbury) and Dunedin (Otago) are exhibiting the same trend of low mean patch size and medium to high patch numbers.

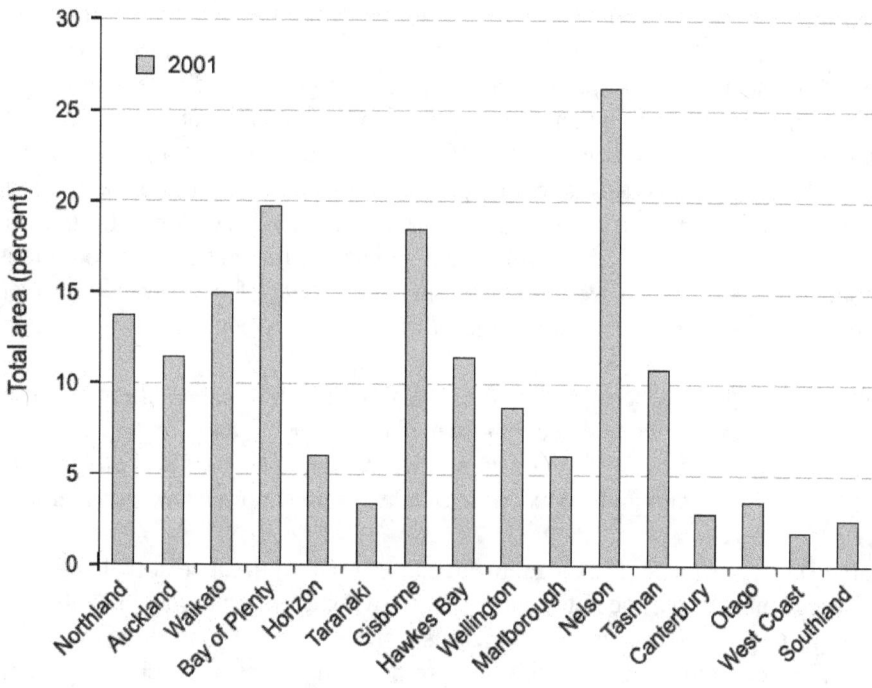

Figure 14—Percentage of total area covered by planted forests by region.

DISCUSSION
Effects of Different Datasets on the Reporting Quality
The comparison of two land classification datasets for the same point in time showed the importance of a high standard of processing and classification. In our case, the main changes were due to a combination of better processing practices and, therefore, more accurate delineation (Miri 2004) but also the better spectral composition of the LANDSAT ETM+ images that were used in Version 2. The example given earlier is the improved segregation of broadleaved hardwoods from planted forests.

The above issue is precisely why the older data were revised, in order that more precise comparisons would be possible between the land covers at the two points of time. As the original land-cover data was used for a number of applications, such as New Zealand's first Montréal report, a comparison of the two 1996 classifications was important to understand the impact of the changes resulting from the revision on derived information. Comparing the first Montréal report with a new one without an understanding of this impact could paint an incorrect picture.

A higher increase in planted forests due to the 13- percent difference between LCDB 1 and LCDB 1v2 (fig. 1) and the decrease of scrubland area because of misclassified broadleaved indigenous hardwoods—which were in fact planted forests—would lead to the wrong assumption that newly planted forests are responsible for the decrease of indigenous scrublands and areas converting back to indigenous forest.

The study shows the need for, and, if possible, the incorporation of error estimates for different datasets over time if such datasets are used for monitoring and tracking changes. There are a number of useful approaches. One way of testing for accuracy is to use better datasets such as aerial photography and ground truthing for areas that are known not to have changed. This method was carried out by Dunningham and others (2000) for LCDB 1. Major misclassifications can be revealed and corrected. For future comparisons, a similar assessment of LCDB 2 would be valuable. Other possible methods include applying the fuzzy set theory (Power and others 2001, DeClercq and DeWulf 2005) or perimeter/area ratios (Salas and others 2003) to correct for differences in data and processing quality.

Heterogeneous Distribution of Forests over the Whole Landscape of New Zealand
The level of reporting on fragmentation that was used for the Montréal report 2003 is probably not sufficient because the patch size distribution of indigenous forests alone can not describe the complexity of fragmentation of forests in a landscape. By reporting at the regional level, the quality of information that can be achieved is of greater value than the reporting on a national level alone and can be used by the regions as strategic information. The occurrence of indigenous and planted forests varied highly at the regional level, and this heterogeneous distribution gives a more accurate picture about the state of forest fragmentation over the landscape. We believe that the details of changes of forest fragmentation are better detected when investigated at the regional level. When comparing the metrics of two regions that differ in total area, the comparison should be used with care (Gustafson 1998). However, by considering the total area of forests and, at times, calculating percentages, differences between the regions can be interpreted.

Another method to detect heterogeneity of forest distribution on a national level is the approach of sampling windows of different sizes to detect landscape heterogeneity, as spatial variation depends on the scale of observation (Gustafson 1998, Löfman and Kouki 2003). Riitters and others (2002) used this approach for the United States and give an example of a large-area approach of this method.

The metrics that we used—percentage of area, mean patch size, and number of patches—are a compromise between being easily understood and still showing a sufficient level of information about forest fragmentation. The decision to use these metrics instead of others that can show a higher strength in characterizing fragmentation is based on this compromise, but future research will investigate the usefulness of other more complex metrics.

RECOMMENDATIONS FOR ECOLOGICAL REPORTING

The Montréal process is aimed at the sustainable management of forests. Key to this is understanding sustainability of forest ecosystems within a country. The analysis of the forests and their fragmentation could be based on the ecological classification of the landscape and metrics used to describe the fragmentation within those physically described ecosystems. This has the advantage in that the amount and the pattern of forests are related to the specific ecological site for a country, and the fragmentation of each ecosystem is known. Specifically, this approach identifies the status of the forests adapted to that environmental situation in terms of occupied area and distribution. The status of key ecological systems and the impact of forest loss can be better highlighted. In New Zealand, we consider two ecological datasets, the Land Environments of New Zealand (LENZ) (Leathwick and others 2002), and the predicted potential natural vegetation of New Zealand (McGlone and others 2004). LENZ is a numerical-based classification of New Zealand's climate, landforms, and soils. The predicted potential natural vegetation is a further development of LENZ, predicting indigenous vegetation-type distribution throughout New Zealand. An example for the use is the depletion of forests in the drier lowland LENZ environment of the eastern South Island within the Canterbury region. Hence, the ecological implications of the remaining forest cover can be better described and interpreted.

CONCLUSIONS

The study showed that there is an increase in forest cover in New Zealand for the period 1996 and 2001. This increase is mainly due to the establishment of new planted forests. Indigenous forests, with their mostly protected status, showed a stable distribution of forest sizes and almost no changes. The distribution of forests varied greatly from region to region, and this would be useful to incorporate in the reporting process to capture a clearer picture for the country, especially when incorporating the ecological environments and the distribution of forest types that depend on special ecosystems. To gain appropriate and sufficiently accurate results in monitoring forest fragmentation, accuracy assessments need to be performed on the underlying datasets. Issues of comparability need to be investigated and, if necessary, an error estimation or correction method applied. In order to facilitate the understanding of the processes fragmenting forests, it is also the aim of future research to incorporate other metrics and investigate the complementarities of indigenous and planted forests in the landscapes of New Zealand.

LITERATURE CITED

Brockerhoff, E.G.; Ecroyd, C.E.; Langer, E.R. 2001. Biodiversity in New Zealand plantation forests: policy trends, incentives, and the state of our knowledge. New Zealand Journal of Forestry. 46: 31-37.

Cain, D.H.; Riitters, K.; Orvis, K. 1997. A multi-scale analysis of landscape statistics. Landscape Ecology. 12: 199-212.

DeClercq, E.M.; DeWulf, R.R. 2005. Probabilistic change detection and fuzzy set theory using historic forest maps. Presentation. Brisbane: IUFRO 2005 conference.

Dunningham, A.G.; Brownlie, R.K.; Firth, J.G. 2000. Classification accuracy of NZLCDB1: results. rotorua, NZ: New Zealand Forest Research Ltd. 63 p. Available from: the Ministry for the Environment.

ESRI. 2004. ARCInfo 9.0. http://www.esri.com. [Date accessed: November 2006]. Software.

Gustafson, E.J. 1998. Quantifying landscape spatial pattern: what is the state of the art. Ecosystems. 1: 143-156.

Harris, L.D. 1984. The fragmented forest: island biogeographic theory and the preservation of biotic diversity. Chicago: University of Chicago Press. 211 p.

Leathwick, J.; Morgan, F.; Wilson, G. [and others]. 2002. Land environments of New Zealand: technical guide. Ministry for the Environment. http://www.mfe.govt nz/publications/ser/lenz-apr03 html. [Date accessed: November 2006].

Löfman, S.; Kouki, J. 2003. Scale and dynamics of a transforming forest landscape. Forest Ecology and Management. 1-3: 247-252. Vol. 175.

McGarigal, K.; Marks, B.J. 1994. FRAGSTATS: spatial pattern analysis program for quantifying landscape structures. Gen. Tech. Rep. PNW-GTR-351. Portland, OR: U.S. Department of Agriculture, Forest Service, Pacific Northwest Research Station. 122 p.

McGarigal, K.; Marks, B.J.; Holmes, C.; Ene, E. 2002. Fragstats 3.3 spatial pattern analysis program for quantifying landscape structures. [Software.]

McGlone, M.S.; Walker, J.; Leathwick, J.F.; Briggs, C. 2004. Predicted potential natural vegetation of New Zealand. New Zealand: Manaaki Whenua Landcare Research. Poster and electronic data. http://www.landcareresearch.co.nz/databases/lenz/products_poster.asp. [Date accessed: November 2006].

Ministry of Agriculture and Forestry. 2002. New Zealand Country Report: Montreal Process Criteria and Indicators for the Conservation and Sustainable Management of Temperate and Boreal Forests 2003. Ministry of Agriculture and Forestry, Wellington, New Zealand.

Miri, S.A. 2004. Image analysis and GIS processing land cover database 2 (LCDB2) Stage 4. Wellington, NZ: Terralink International Ltd. 13 p.

Neel, M.C.; McGarigal, K.; Cushman, S.A. 2004. Behavior of class-level landscape metrics across gradients of class aggregation and area. Landscape Ecology. 19: 435-455.

New Zealand Ministry of Agriculture and Forestry. 2003. Montréal Country Report 2003. 156 p. http://www.maf.govt.nz/forestry/montreal-process/nz-country-rpt-2003.pdf. [Date accessed: November 2006].

Power, C.; Simms, A.; White, R. 2001. Hierarchical fuzzy pattern matching for the regional comparison of land use maps. International Journal of Geographical Information Science. 15: 77-100.

Riitters, K.H.; Wickham, J.D.; O'Neill, R.V.; Jones, K.B.; Smith, E.R.; Coulston, J.W.; Wade, T.G.; Smith, J.H. 2002. Fragmentation of continental United States forests. Ecosystems. 5: 815-822.

Salas, W.; Boles, S.; Frolking, S. [and others]. 2003. The perimeter/area ratio as an index of misregistration bias in land cover change estimates. International Journal of Remote Sensing. 24: 3311-3340.

Statistics New Zealand. 2001. Statistics by area. http://www.stats.govt nz/. [Date accessed: November 2006].

Thompson, S.; Gruner, I.; Gapare, N. 2003. New Zealand land cover database. Version 2. Illustrated guide to target classes. Technical user guide. Version 4.0._April 2004. Ministry for the Environment. http://www mfe.govt nz/issues/land/land-cover-dbase/. [Date accessed: November 2006].

IMPLEMENTATION OF THE MCPFE INDICATOR "FOREST SPATIAL PATTERN" TO REPORT ON EUROPEAN FOREST BIODIVERSITY

Peter Vogt, Christine Estreguil, and Jacek Kozak[1]

Abstract—The first results of a new method designed to classify and analyze forest spatial pattern from forest maps derived from satellite imagery are described in this paper. The approach preserves the knowledge of the neighborhood context and classifies the forest map into the six forest classes: perforated, edge, patch, core, branch, and corridor. The conceptual ideas are summarized and demonstrated at country level for European states. The temporal evolution of forest spatial pattern is investigated at local scale for a Natura2000 site in northern Italy. The impact of both the selected classification unit and the initial forest map on the classification result is addressed.

INTRODUCTION

The monitoring and reporting on the status and evolution of European forest biodiversity has become one of the key components of the European Union's policy on Environment and Sustainable Development, affecting, for example, the Forest Focus Regulation and the Habitat and Bird Directives (EU 1992). At the European Stakeholders Conference in Malahide (Malahide Conference 2004), 15 biodiversity headline indicators were adopted including "trends in extent of selected biomes, ecosystems and habitats" and "connectivity/fragmentation of ecosystems." The conservation of forest biodiversity has led to international protocols for monitoring forest habitats including the area of forest by forest types and its spatial pattern (MPLO 2000, MCPFE 2005). Sustainable forest management and trend analysis of forest biodiversity therefore require precise mapping and statistics of forest spatial pattern. Remote sensing is a practical way to obtain consistent data for forest area (Estreguil and others 2003, Estreguil and others 2004, Innes and Koch 1998, Koch and Ivits 2004) and for the retrieval of biodiversity-relevant information on forest composition and structure at the land cover and landscape levels. Continental land cover maps have been used to map forest extent (GAF 2001, Hame and others 2001, I&CLC 2000) and to quantify and map forest fragmentation (Puumalainen and others 2003, Uuttera and others 2003). Numerous metrics have been proposed and computed over selected test sites, but no common monitoring system for forest structure on large areas has yet been presented. Neel and others (2004) suggest that most indices are correlated with forest area, and Riitters and others (1995) demonstrated that the information obtained from 50 indices can be described with six parameters alone. Here, we discuss the detection and quantification of the six forest spatial pattern classes—core, patch, edge, perforated, branch, and corridor—from binary forest–nonforest maps derived from the CORINE Land Cover database and Landsat satellite imagery of the years 1987 and 2000.

METHODS AND APPLICATION

A classification scheme to describe forest spatial pattern is derived from a binary forest–nonforest mask. This mask can be directly derived from satellite data (Landsat, Image2000) or through re-classification of land cover data such as the Corine land cover data set. Originally designed by Riitters and others (2000), the classification process was amended by Vogt and others (2006) with morphological filtering techniques to classify the pixels of the raster input image into the following six classes:

1. Core: center and all neighbor pixels have the same attribute
2. Patch: coherent region of forest without core forest
3. Edge: pixels separating core forest and core nonforest

---

[1] Peter Vogt, Christine Estreguil, Jacek Kozak, European Commission - DG Joint Research Centre, Institute for Environment and Sustainability, Land Management and Natural Hazards Unit, Ispra, Italy.

4. Perforated: forested outside border of nonforest patch
5. Corridor: pixels connecting core forested regions
6. Branch: pixels branching off from core forest regions

A graphical illustration of the classifiers is shown in on the left side of figure 1 for a sample forest mask. The top half of this figure shows the two versions of the Structuring Element (SE) used in this study. In essence, morphological filtering is designed to find (or remove) the user-defined SE in the image. The method provides a computationally efficient way for the automatic classification of forest spatial pattern. Figure 2 displays regional-level results over Slovakia on the basis of a forest mask with a spatial resolution of 100 m. A subset of this image shows forested corridors along a river between two mountainous regions. The whole country was classified on a standard PC in 12 seconds. At the local level, the method was applied to the Val Grande National Park (http://www.parks.it/parco.nazionale.valgrande/Eindex.html) in northern Italy. With a size of 14 600 ha, this park is part of the Natura2000 network

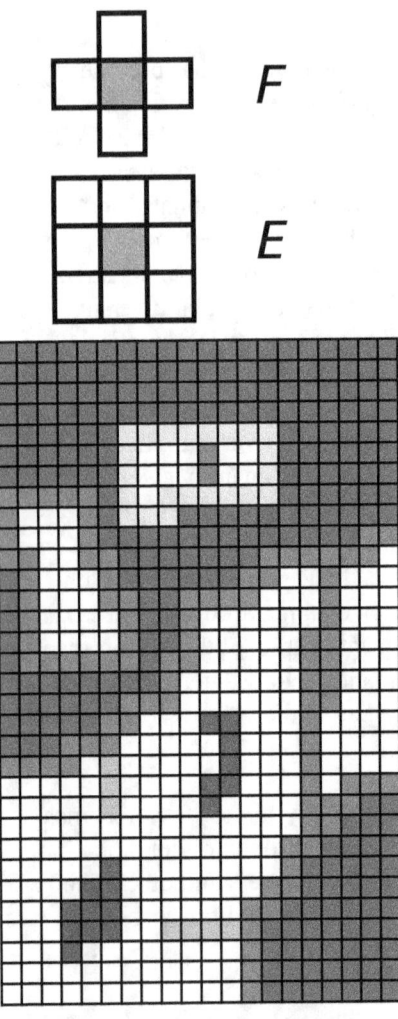

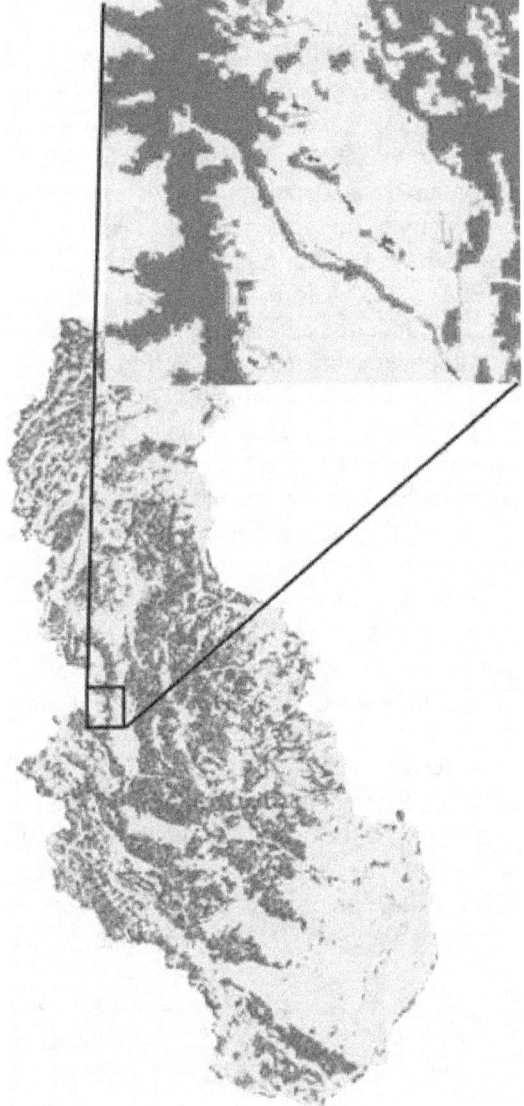

Figure 1—Bottom: Thematic definition of forest spatial pattern pixel classifiers: core—green, edge—red, patch—blue, perforated—yellow, branch—cyan, corridor—magenta. Top: The two structuring elements (SEs) used: E (eight-connected) and F (four-connected). Squares represent the pixels belonging to the SE with the center pixel highlighted in grey.

Figure 2—Western Carpathians, Tatra Mountains and Liptov Basin: Corridors along river valleys connecting separated mountainous regions.

and has been protected since 1967. Landsat satellite data for the years 1985 and 2000 were analyzed, and forest and transitional woodland were included to make the forest masks for each year. The pattern classification results for this particular site indicate an increase in core forest and patch size due to land abandonment and invasion processes (fig. 3).

The classification results mainly depend on the input forest mask and the size of the structuring element used in the analysis. The variety of thematic and spatial detail of the forest map is illustrated in figure 4. For the same region, two forest masks were derived, one from the Corine land cover data set (100 m) and one from Landsat 7 satellite data (25 m). With 44 land cover classes, Corine provides a unique Europe-wide and harmonized land cover product. Its spatial resolution is, however, about one-fourth as detailed as a Landsat-based land cover classification. Forest maps derived from high spatial resolution satellite data provide better insight into the complex pattern of forest and are more suited for European pattern analysis. They reveal more spatial detail of small-scale features like small forest patches or nonforest openings and corridors within apparently homogenous forest areas. The analysis with morphological filters uses a structuring element of predefined size and dimension. The default settings apply a kernel or window of 3 by 3 pixels to classify at pixel level. An increase in the size of the structuring element will increase the width of all classifiers but core. It may also change the classification for a small region; for example, a small core forest area with edge will turn into a patch when analysed with a larger structuring element. The impact of this effect is shown in figure 5 for the Val Grande National Park.

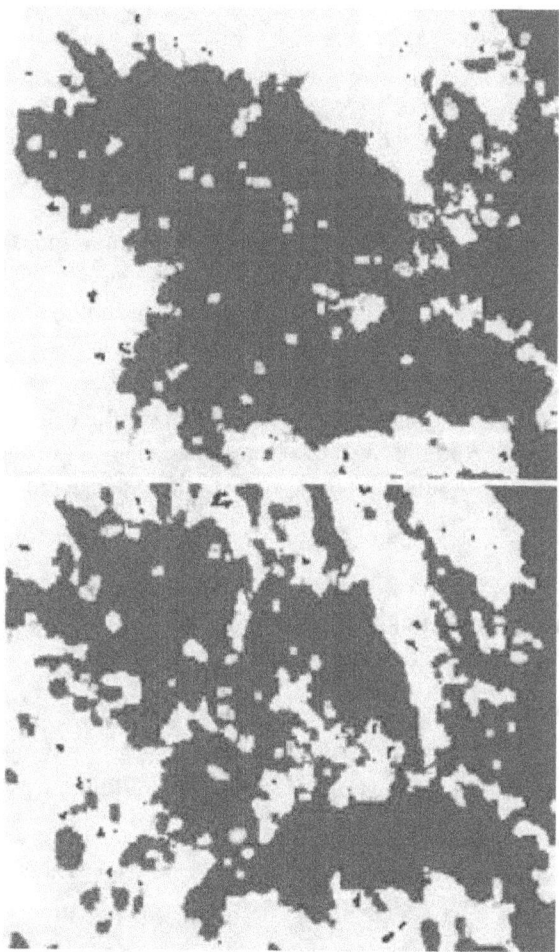

Figure 3—Increase of core forest in Val Grande National Park, northern Italy, years 1985 to 2000.

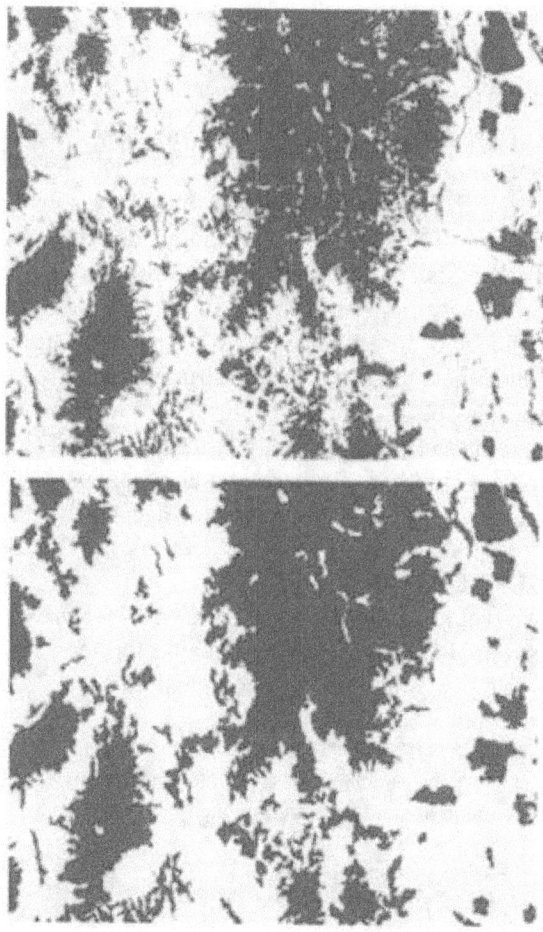

Figure 4—Variety in thematic and spatial detail of the derived input forest mask (~ 20 by 23 km): from Corine LC with 44 land cover classes and 100-m spatial resolution (left) and from Landsat 7 with only three forest-type classes but 28-m spatial resolution (right).

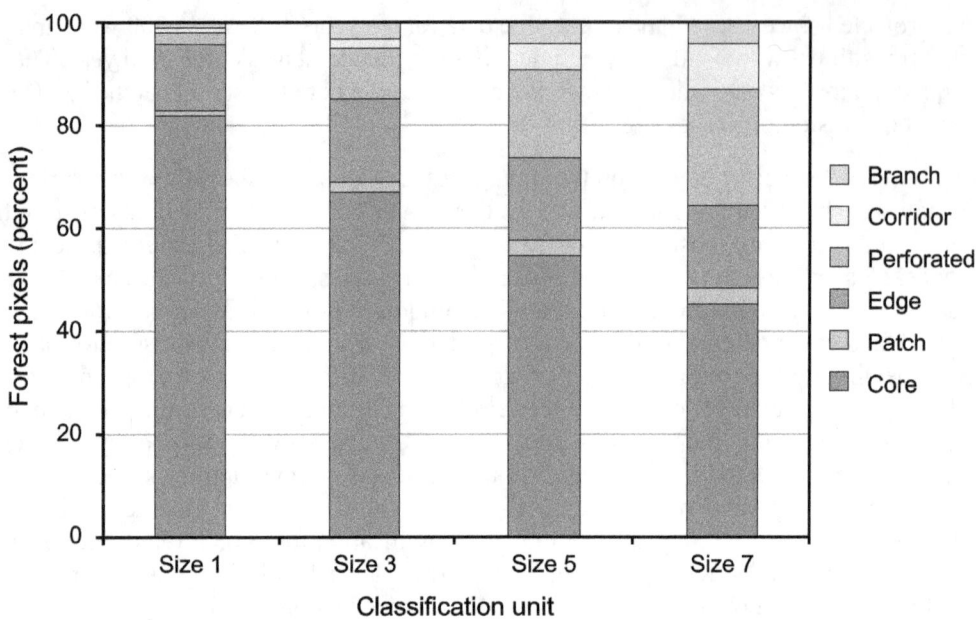

Figure 5—Classification results as a function of the selected classification unit (size of the structuring element).

RESULTS

The proposed classification scheme provides an efficient way to map and measure six ecologically relevant forest spatial pattern classes. This evaluation can be performed on different spatial scales as well as for different times allowing for trend analysis and monitoring of the effectiveness of environmental policies. The classifiers are intuitive and descriptive and are provided on the same scale as the input map. The consistent visual approach allows for statistical analysis in time and space. Existing parameters often provide a single statistic measure for a given region. In contrast, our method describes the geographic variance of forest attributes, which is mandatory for trend analysis. The classification results are a function of the user-selected structuring element. This flexibility can be used to obtain predefined, species-specific width of forest edges and corridors. In the future, studies on the pattern classes, their relation to the reality on the ground, and their integration into ecologically scaled landscape analysis need to be conducted. Further research will address additional metrics/indicators for forest spatial pattern and connectivity and their capacity to accurately map changes over time.

ACKNOWLEDGMENTS

We would like to thank Marco Cerruti for providing data and in-depth knowledge about the Val Grande National Park. Many special thanks to Pierre Soille and Marcin Iwanowski from JRC/LMU for the in-depth discussion on morphological image processing techniques.

LITERATURE CITED

EU. 1992. Council Directive 92/43/EEC 21 May 1992. Conservation of natural habitats and of wild fauna and flora. Brussels: Commission of European Communities.

Estreguil, C.M.; Deshayes, M.; Lamb, A. [and others]. 2003. Indicators for biodiversity and nature protection. A contribution JRC European Commission publ. reference EUR 20861/EN.

Estreguil, C.M.; Cerruti, M. 2004. Portfolio of earth observation based indicators for biodiversity and nature protection. EUR 21078/EN.

GAF. 2001. IRS WIFS image mosaic classification of forest classes for the European Union (EU15). Final report. Contract Nr17240-2000-12F1ED ISP DE. 17.06.2001. JRC–European Commission. 26 p.

Hame, T.; Stenberg, P.; Andersson, K. [and others]. 2001. AVHRR-based forest proportion map of Pan European area. Remote sensing of environment. 77: 66-91.

Innes, J.L.; Koch, B. 1998. Forest biodiversity and its assessment by remote sensing. Global Ecology and Biogeography Letters. 7(6): 397-419.

I&CLC. 2000. [The Image & Corine Land Cover] 2000 database. http://terrestrial.eionet.eu.int/CLC2000 and http://image2000.jrc.it/.

Koch, B.; Ivits, E. 2004. Results from the project bioassess- relation between remote sensing and terrestrial derived biodiversity indicators. In: Marchetti, M., ed. Monitoring and indicators of forest biodiversity in Europe: from ideas to operationality. EFI Proceedings 51. European Forest Institute: 316-332.

Malahide Conference 2004. 'Message from Malahide' from the stakeholder's conference entitled 'Biodiversity and the EU - sustaining life, sustaining livelihoods' held under the Irish Presidency in Malahide, Ireland, from 25th to 27th May 2004. http://biodiversity-chm.eea.europa.eu/stories/STORY1087980667.

MCPFE 2005. MCPFE Work Programme: Pan-European follow-up of the fourth ministerial conference on the protection of forests in Europe, Liaison Unit. Warsaw, Warszawa, Poland. http://www.mcpfe.org/publications/pdf/.

MPLO. 2000. Progress and innovation in implementing criteria and indicators for the conservation and sustainable management of temperate and boreal forests. Montréal process year 2000 progress rep. Ottawa, Canada: The Montréal Process Liaison Office, Canadian Forest Service.

Neel, M.C.; McGarigal, K.; Cushman, S.A. 2004. Behavior of class-level landscape metrics across gradients of class aggregation and area. Landscape Ecology. 19: 435-455.

Puumalainen, J.; Kennedy, P.; Folving, S. 2003. Monitoring forest biodiversity: a European perspective with reference to temperate and boreal forest zone. Journal of Environmental Management. Vol. 67(1): 1-27. [Special issue: Maintaining Forest Biodiversity].

Riitters, K.H.; O'Neill, R.; Hunsaker, C. [and others]. 1995. A factor analysis of landscape pattern and structure metrics. Landscape Ecology. 10(1): 23-39.

Riitters, K.H.; Wickham, J.; O'Neill, R. [and others]. 2000. Global-scale patterns of forest fragmentation. Conservation Ecology. 4(2): 3. http://www.ecologyandsociety.org/vol4/iss2/art3/.

Uuttera, J.; Folving, S.; Kennedy, P.; Puumalainen, J. 2003. Monitoring forest landscape diversity at European level: case studies on forest types and fragmentation. JRC European Commission publ. ref. EUR 20740 EN.

Vogt, P.; Riitters, K.H.; Estreguil, C. [and others]. 2006. Mapping spatial patterns with morphological image processing. Landscape Ecology. 22: 171-177., DOI: 10.1007/s10980-006-9013-2.